# Imagine That

JUDITH O'CONNELL HOYER

FUTURECYCLE PRESS
*www.futurecycle.org*

Cover artwork by Robert Weiss; author photo by Sarah Ricardi; interior
and cover design by Diane Kistner; Adobe Garamond Pro text and Avenir Next
Condensed titling

Library of Congress Control Number: 2022950375

Published by FutureCycle Press
Athens, Georgia, USA

ISBN 978-1-952593-42-0

"A poem is never finished, only abandoned."

—Paul Valery

*for* RICHARD, *always*

# Contents

**ONE**

Wedding Day Photo.................................................................11
Allied Bombs Hit Foe in France Hard........................................12
Wonder................................................................................13
Evening Bag...........................................................................14
Tempus Fugit.........................................................................15
Great-Aunts...........................................................................16
Tulips...................................................................................17
A Natural..............................................................................18
Scent of Lilacs.......................................................................19
The Long Ride.......................................................................20
End of Childhood..................................................................21
Paris....................................................................................22
Room 431.............................................................................23
Leave-Taking.........................................................................24
On Her Last Afternoon...........................................................26

**TWO**

Lost Landscapes.....................................................................29
I'm Talking to You..................................................................30
Heirloom..............................................................................31
Inheritance............................................................................32
Voices..................................................................................33
What Keeps Me Going............................................................34
One Day................................................................................35
While You Were Away.............................................................36
Hope....................................................................................37
Grace...................................................................................38
Easter Morning......................................................................39
Pentecost Sunday in Norway....................................................40
Scenes from Zagreb................................................................42
Vancouver Hatchery...............................................................43
Anticipation..........................................................................44
Picking Concord Grapes..........................................................45
Garter Snake.........................................................................46
My Friend and I.....................................................................47
Praise Song...........................................................................48

On the Metro-North from New Haven....................................................49
Imagination...............................................................................................50
Root Canal................................................................................................51
Mohs Surgery, or Gentle on My Mind...................................................52

## THREE

Imagine That............................................................................................55
Day before Thanksgiving..........................................................................56
Therapy......................................................................................................57
Spring Chaos.............................................................................................58
Talking to Nature......................................................................................59
The NewsHour...........................................................................................60
Aubade.......................................................................................................61
Finding Love in the Laundry Room.........................................................62
End of Wandering.....................................................................................63
Who I Am..................................................................................................64
Sitting at the Beach...................................................................................65
This Present Life........................................................................................66
Looking Back.............................................................................................68
Women Friends..........................................................................................69

# ONE

## *Wedding Day Photo*

—April 30, 1943

It's a Kodak catch outside Llano's Barber and Beauty Shop,
as they leave barbered and viewed seriously beautiful.

Prickly hairs attack his neck.
A nest of Aleutian curls blazes around her face.

Noon heaps no safety on their brows
as they squint into a vast and pounding sun.

Thirteen formidable buttons guard the bride's modesty.
Her clutch hides a supply of melting lipstick,

bobby pins and Wednesday's ticket stub
punched by a conductor in far-flung Eastern Standard Time.

A private salutes the couple en route to the chapel
where potted Easter lilies substitute for wedding guests.

Airy blue petals decorate her shoulder.
Khakis are his required complement.

Pure *I do's* echo through empty pews
while jeeps vroom by the perimeter.

After settling for a Texas roadhouse pork chop special,
they strike out into Midland's incendiary heat

and swallow kisses like Karo syrup on a spoon,
deaf to bombers' moon-lit runs.

May 5th's dreaded Okinawa orders are slashed
when he is fever-hit and hospitalized.

# Allied Bombs Hit Foe in France Hard

—*New York Times* front page story 2/10/1944

It was a straighten-up-and-fly-right birth,
a Kodak first-day snap of me in my mother's arms,
set free in Texas heat, an onslaught that
began before dawn and cooled down under

waning moonlight as Allied forces raked
a railroad junction, and then everything
was square in Midland and Limoges with kisses
planted like bombs by the Brits flying low
who plastered the Nazi engine works.

Only one pilot failed to return, and it was
not he whom she counted on to arrive
home from work at eight minutes past five,
who listened to *Too-Ra-Loo-Ra-Loo-Ra*
while he ate his skinless franks and baked beans.

## *Wonder*

Forsythia buds had yet to swell.
      March, when I was five.
Beyond, out there, where only kids went,
      two men in singlets and boxer shorts
dashed, one behind the other into the woods.
      Nothing I had ever seen.
Spare as saplings, they stung the undergrowth
      with switches stripped from hanging branches
frantic to escape the yelp of hounds.
      Now my mother, out of reach,
leans against the porcelain sink,
      water running hard to fill a pot.
She does not sense the wonder
      that holds me firm against the glass.
My eyes open on a brook, bare trees, brush,
      and those bodies on air.
Things I dare not share with her.

## Evening Bag

Its brass frame opens wide
like an eye eager to examine whatever drops inside:
a nickel for lemonade, dance card, hairpin.

An enveloping skin of creamy beads
is seeded around the withered handiwork
of embroidered rosebuds, daisies, and silk bows.

There's a hole in the lining the size of a white lie
my grandmother might have told her mother
about what happened that night.

It's been kept since the prom when it hung
by its chain on the back of her chair
as she waltzed onto the dance floor

in his arms, "Down by the Old Mill Stream,"
where the air was out of breath and her
elaborate coil of hair was coming undone.

## Tempus Fugit

My grandmother caught me preening
in her bedroom mirror at the rest home

where I worked as a teenage nurse's aide,
*a proud haughty* in my red-checked shirtwaist,

delivering triangles of egg salad sandwiches
and tiny pots of lukewarm tea to the old ladies.

I can see her hands, the way she'd fold them
in her lap, the way she'd squeeze her fingers tight,

then relax them like the corroded rhythms of her heart.
I was allowed to bring her digitalis

that rolled inside a paper cup, black as mold.
I'd tip the stimulant into her open palm.

She'd throw her head back and down it dry.
I have her gold lady's watch with its balky minute hand

engraved in elegant scrolls by a jeweler in Waltham.
I wear it with endless pleasure on a chain around my neck.

On the back of the case is a bird,
its wings unfurled in flight.

## Great-Aunts

Inherited the house their father built
with a garage out back for the Buick where
ghosts babbled rose dust in the garden.

Handsome Misses with hair crimped in post-war do's
and huge bosoms passed down by their mother.
They puffed pink cigarettes but never inhaled and

dabbed sweat with crocheted hankies stuffed in sleeves.
Breakfast was bowls of harlequin ice cream.
When I got engaged, Belle asked, *Where's he from?*

*Hear that, Agnes? She had to go*
*all the way to St. Louis to find a husband.*
During Advent, Grace made the magi cross

the Oriental, inch by inch, day by day
to the crèche camped on the hearth,
where they arrived on January 6th.

## Tulips

My mother told me years later that when she bent down to grab
     a damp sheet from the basket to hang on the line,
I was standing there clutching tulips
     she knew were from Greta Walker's garden.
I imagine them red, five or six at most,
     their heads nodding this way and that,
a few leaning over at the waist.
     She said Greta was on her knees weeping.
I assume my mother tried to comfort her
     then lifted me up and away,
petals dropping in our wake.
     Greta died of cancer not long after
leaving Steven, who was tall and once
     took me to the prom in his father's Ford sedan.
I remember my mother's surprise when she had to look up at us.
     Me in lime sherbet. Spiked heels dyed to match.
Wrist banded with daisies that would rest
     on the shoulder of his tweed jacket
as we slow-danced in the school gym that night.
     Another May is here strewn with violets in the grass.
I'll pick as many as I can before the mower takes them down.

## A Natural

I remember the '55 Buick Special in the driveway, still.
　　My father is down to an undershirt, khakis belted,
　　　　cuffs turned to the ankles, old brogues on asphalt.
From his neck swings a medal of the Virgin Mary.
　　He nods to me crouching on the banking.
　　　　In a pail of lukewarm suds, he drowns a brown sponge.
Hauls the thing back up from the sea where it's been
　　hiding in the dark like a childhood memory.
　　　　Carries it, heavy, to the roof. Swabs the length of the car
back to front, front to back, always returning to the source
　　for more to soothe hood, glass, doors, fenders, bumpers, hubcaps.
　　　　Each lithe movement choreographed
to the sounds of water. All of it so like him.
　　After the hose-down, he reaches for the chamois cloth
　　　　that drapes his back pocket.
I watch him make each bead of water vanish.
　　Only now do I recall winter days, hands frozen from outside play,
　　　　when he'd place one hand flat against my palm,
the other on the back side, and rub until I could feel the heat.
　　Then he'd start on the other hand.

## Scent of Lilacs

Arthur Faucher
was there
when I was.
Lilacs someone
brought to school
made him wheeze,
made him sick.
Brought him down
beside an elm
when he fell behind
the patrol line.
He is gone,
yet every May
the scent is back
to second grade,
to those blossoms
shaped like lungs,
to Miss Gilligan
leaning over my desk
with her sharp pencil
teaching me
how to subtract.

## The Long Ride

We were waiting in front
of Barnard Department Store
when the #19 Burncoat
dumped its air at the curb.
You hustled on and sat
facing me. The Paramount sliding
off to the right, Burns Spa, North Park.
No frayed algebra on your lap,
no varsity jacket to call you out,
no steady's ring to fidget with your thumb,
no Wrigley's Spearmint
to snap between your teeth,
no smokes in the shirt pocket
of your blue button-down,
no tip-offs in a brown bag beside you,
just that scar beneath your eye.
At Quinapoxet Lane you played
the cord above your head,
lurched side to side,
a pinball caroming toward its target.
I saw you grab the driver's bag of cash and
make a dash into a Worcester zip code
of flopping towels and overalls,
privet hedges, backyard toolsheds.
On that long ride your eyes
never met my gaze.
You were tough to figure out, like X.
Tell me how you got that scar.
Tell me what you spent the money on.

## End of Childhood

I was a believer in those honest acres inside
invisible gates where I ran, sunny and solitary,
from my mother's unforeseeable moods.

Where my feet pumped high over the caretaker's
cottage, summer house and swimming rink.
Beyond everything, Green Hill, and the buffalo.

Where a grand fountain cooled down geraniums,
the earth around, the wire surround and boys
on bikes who rode too close.

Where carp with mouths as wide as galvanized pails
rose empty from the fishpond underworld
to fill on bread pilfered from the pantry.

Where I learned to fringe a linen placemat with
the feel and color of parakeet feathers that cushioned
my breakfast cereal, banana, and spoon.

Where the facts of life were blabbed to me
on a stone bridge that led from before to after.
There weren't many words, and the girl was gone.

Where I can still hear a horseshoe striking
luck around a metal stake or landing
with a thunk in a cloud of red dirt.

## *Paris*

I learned how to eat
that summer
on the Left Bank.

New to me
were bowls of tea
to wallow in.
So I let myself go.

I'd never experienced
a mash of orange in a glass
that blossomed
where it willed.

Croissants
eased apart like
a woman's hands unfolding,
tender as a promise.

Tiny pots of yogurt
lacquered sweet—
nothing my mouth
had ever known.

On a bench
in the Parc Montsouris,
we'd slip slices of peach
into open baguettes.

With every crunch,
juice would find our clothes,
our arms, our legs.

The day we had to part,
stars plunged
into Parisian soil

like herbs buried in a cassoulet.

## Room 431

So this is where you've been—in your get-well room
asking God for another chance.
*Cool as a cucumber,* says the nurse,
referring to your temperature, while outside
bodies are sweating like cheese in the heat.

Our two heads turn toward your hospital bed.
Tabletop foam sticks bend your way. *Sip,* they lisp.
A silver, beetle-shiny, swivel-footed dribbler
tips nutrient into you every five seconds.

Spasms from yesterday's gastric bypass cause
your torso to crush as an empty can of Diet Coke would.
You are wild for the next hit of something under lock and key,
something to make you feel serene and incurious.

Then there's the pink balloon with its grocery store barcode
bought on the fly by yesterday's visitor from church,
a gift that reminds me of your stomach filled with air,
unable to work on a bowl of creamy mac and cheese.

Now the inflated greeting is offering the slightest royal wave
egged-on by the AC that can hardly suppress a breezy tee-hee,
which brings to mind the boxes of blue latex protectors on the wall
marked S, M and L that will applaud when you're better and ready for home.

## Leave-Taking

This is how he dies: in the living room,
in a hospital bed, taking in the map of Belgium
hung over the fireplace fifty years ago.
Her country, where they met.

He is under glass, too.
*Don't touch!* the hospice nurse says.
*It hurts. Touch hurts,*
*except his forehead.*

And this is how he goes: eyes keen
on his brother's words as he recalls
the Remington mower their dad bought
when they lived on Puritan Circle in Springfield.

*It was so hard to push,* my husband says.
We understand the whispered *yes.*
*But the blades spun fast,*
*giving the grass a neat even cut.*

Your email says that you move from room to room
removing his things one at a time, hanger by hanger.
I imagine you pitching prescription bottles, wallet,
eyeglasses, passport, carton of peach ice cream.

It is not what you are looking for,
it's what you find—the risk of being busy,
a risky business after all.
The certainty, the uncertainty of it all.

From the front door you do a double take,
catch a glimpse of him gabbing with the neighbor
who's returning an adjustable wrench he borrowed
last month for some kind of car fix.

Tricked, you slam the god-damned door,
bolt for your room, and drop into oblivion.

Hours later you come alive to the roar of a mower
being pushed across someone else's yard,

its sharp blade cutting one swath after another,
leaving you with the smell of grass trying to save itself.

## On Her Last Afternoon

—In memory of Janice Reidy, 1911-2018

She pats the hospital bed. She wants me to sit.
With help, she maneuvers the flexible straw

that sprouts from a carton of milk
and into her mouth through an opening in her oxygen mask.

*It's so cold. It tastes so good. It's good for me.* Then she adds,
*I want to hear all about your trip to London.*

Like the air she is so desperate for,
she takes in everything: drafty Westminster Abbey,

choir boys in scarlet cassocks topped with pleated white collars,
the scissored acres of Greenwich where locals run their dogs,

and the 50th anniversary couple from the Isle of Jersey
we met on the observation deck of The Shard.

She says, *The Germans occupied the Channel Islands during the war.
Sark and Guernsey are two of them.* And she's right!

I tell her about the glass-domed lobby of the St. Pancras Hotel
where tea and scones are served on silver trays and
linen napkins are folded like wallets.

*There are two railway stations there,* she says, right again.

So agog is she despite woolly vision, worn-down hearing,
blue fingertips, her masked dry mouth and nose.

Outside the window, snow squalls cut to chilled rain.

*It's so cold. It tastes so good,* she says.

# TWO

## Lost Landscapes

because my mother trimmed string beans with a wooden-handled knife she gripped with her left hand, each cut making tiny plinks in the bottom of the pot

because the remedy for colon cancer is a warm compress prepared by a third-year medical student that drips into my ears and onto the pillow of the hospital bed

because this is a candid shot of my Great-Aunt Liz in her heyday, arms akimbo in a dropped-waist outfit bought in a boutique near the Tuileries for two dollars

because a woman I met at the drugstore while I was waiting for a prescription told me that her husband never lived to learn that their son died of a heroin overdose on the streets of Bellows Falls

because I am the only one left who heard my mother slap her sister's cheek in the middle of the kitchen on the day my grandfather was buried

because I am the interlocutor between my great-grandfather's orchard that no longer blooms on Garfield Street and the peck of apples on my cutting board

because it is possible to float on your back, read *The Telegram,* and smile while drawing a crowd on the shores of Lake Quinsigamond

because the opal-green hummingbird at my feeder dribbling sugar water from his implausibly long beak has a plan for Panama coming up at the end of this week

## I'm Talking to You

Grandmother's mahogany end tables,
my other grandmother's fluted vase,
Aunt Marge's petit point-covered side chair,
and the O'Connell family Bible
rescued from the house on Garfield Street
after the hurricane in '55.
You've been around for generations.
I've done my bit to keep you on, and
I'm just about at the end of my rope.
It's high time you stopped
the back talk, silent treatment,
put-downs, dirty Irish tricks.
No more remarks about what irks you,
who mimics you, mocks you,
turns their back on you,
avoids you on the street.
Look at me.
I'm on to you,
you end tables,
you vase,
you side chair,
you Bible.

## Heirloom

For 40 years
the Limoges serving piece
rimmed with tiny pink roses
sat out-of-round behind
the breakfront's glass doors.
Whenever my foot landed,
coming or going,
between dining room and kitchen,
it would be my Great-Aunt Liz rattling on,
*I was at a party*
*sitting on a man's lap, and*
*he squeezed me so tight*
*he broke one of my ribs.*
No placing it this way or that,
no matchbook cover nudged underneath,
no amount of coaxing made the story cease.
I kept that platter used for
sliced white and dark, legs, wings,
and the pope's nose,
that part of the bird's behind
she'd claim every Thanksgiving Day,
her fingers and mouth all greasy
with the pleasure of it.

## Inheritance

It's nothing you get from walking in the woods.
No asking Google *Why me?*
*A change in the DNA from one generation to the next*
is what the oncologist said to me.
The tumor is gone now.
Two permanent ink spots on my backside,
an empty double port on my chest above my heart,
and a silver line that runs
from my navel to the top of my pubic bone—
things that were left to me.
I'm reading *Great Expectations* for a second time.
Yesterday I bought two pairs of heels instead of one.
I'm not sending Christmas cards this year.
Blessings in disguise.

## *Voices*

The needle drops in place
and the sound is static-free
on the gramophone of memory.
I listen to them say the same old things,
in the same old calico-printed housedresses,
in the same old slipcovered wing chairs,
in the same old clapboard houses,
in the same old part of town.
Alone in my grandmother's pantry,
I pry open the lid with cookies inside.
What was easy to remove was impossible to replace.

## What Keeps Me Going

I cry behind the wheel of my car.
Little red flags flutter in my belly.
I read articles that fail to make sense
of consequences that wear black and white.
I take my brother to Herbie's
where decisions are grilled.
*A hamburger—no onions.*

Glad for the nearness of strangers,
I wait on a folding chair to donate
O negative in a cold hall with
bad lighting, kind nurses,
needle pricks, tincture of iodine.

At a marquetry exhibit I fall
for a lone Great Blue Heron
whose yellow eye seems to be
searching for what to do next.

Gorgeous trees backlit by sun,
middle schoolers peddling grapefruit,
and construction detours in our village
puncture the skin of my dysphoria.

I muster salt pork, vinegar, onions, beef
for a stew that keeps me on my feet.

## One Day

In the backyard, plastic toys erupt like invasive species.
       A pinwheel leans into the koi pond and frets.
The squirrels are all professional diggers with both paws
       under frost-like dew, frantic to find their cache.
We drum fingers waiting for the throat culture
       to prove the truth of strep in Henry
who lies anonymous among the sofa cushions,
       a soupy bowl of Häagen-Dazs Vanilla by his side.
His dad's sleeves turned back just so. He crushes ice,
       clicks on Pokémon cartoons, feeds the hungry Lab.
Waits for night to sweep in and put things right.

## While You Were Away

I can't stop my tears, but I had fun buying fat oranges for lunch. They peel like bananas and taste like paradise.

I dropped a three-inch wire bike into a tabletop forest of dwarf pine trees and gave it a path to wheel through.

I fed your sleepy Mimosa plant with an eyedropper, as if it were a newborn rabbit abandoned by its mother.

I tucked fruit slices in the pantry: lemon, lime, cherry, orange grape, no watermelon.

I walked alone in the rain, hands free.

I got lost in a *New Yorker* short story about a drifter befriended by a creepy woman who eventually drives the teenager back to her dad's place in New Mexico.

I picked sprigs of pink and white ground cover that shows itself outside your apartment.

I found the jade bowl decorated with pandas for good luck and placed the peppermint-colored sprigs in, one at a time. They should last long after you get back from work on Friday.

I left the apartment key in the pewter jar on top of the bookcase.

## *Hope*

In a downpour chattering the pavement of Midtown,
it is everything to be here with you:

to walk, to take in the slick spectacle
that's in the here,

to hear in the good wet of the dash
the jabber-joy of passersby,

to hope that danger has been stayed
for a few months, a few years,

as we zigzag south, dreaming of
coffee with cream in porcelain cups

in the atrium of a mansion turned museum where
beauty has been bought, borrowed, and hauled inside.

## Grace

Some might believe that grace is in the posture of this spine-straight, silent pilgrim. Some would argue it to be her smooth, sculpture-worthy patina. They'd say it's like the vision of an angel cast in solid brass, the way it clashes with the orange and pink Dunkin' sign on the wall behind her where she sits, plastic sacks fixed at her feet like marble altar stones. Some would consider her grace to be the fact that she is unembarrassed by her dog-bed-of-a-woolen-coat. She is certainly a modest woman who would choose to cover herself with the navy blue of a man's oversized giveaway. Others would suggest that grace is in her polite eyes that rarely blink, that never inspect her hands, that she never minds a strand of hair that gets in her face. Most would notice the elderly couple sipping coffee, the folks in line ready to order from the all-day breakfast menu. She is not interested in them, in food. She replies *no, thank you* to everything except the *coffee, six sugars, one cream* I place in front of her, which she does not touch. Truthfully, it is the onset of the shop's closing when Grace will be swept into tomorrow, when Grace will have to stand, balance her bagged belongings, place one foot in front of the other to avoid a puddle, a pothole, a car, to find shelter on this night that promises a patient rain.

## Easter Morning

I go outside in my bathrobe
to collect colored Wiffle balls,
pick violets that stretch across the lawn,
yawning satisfaction,
purple and white ones my grandson ate.
I told him he could.
Inside it's one step by land,
ten by sea, and I'm in the bedroom—
reining in Paul Revere's mare,
harvesting Mr. Potato Head's lips and tongue,
ejecting the kinged and the cornered
from their playing field,
crating a green dinosaur
the size of a newborn—
when on the floor I spy with my little eye
a red die with four white pips.
So much depends on luck.
Now I'm vacuuming coconut
from the dining room rug,
gathering up yesterday's jackets and
five-fingered mittens—
things people leave behind,
like the ironstone turkey platter
that endured an Atlantic crossing in 1858,
the one with a small imperfection,
a brown stain in the glaze.

## Pentecost Sunday in Norway

Far from the city,
rain continues its fall from
spire to streets, empty

'til the smart and lean
emerge from cars with little
need for gasoline.

Church doors are wedged wide.
Organ jubilant—on its
feet. I slip inside.

No infant bawling,
impatient to be named—no
bride's calm maid mending

veiled anxiety.
*Lov Gud* the chorus wills a
gathered laity.

Wives in cropped-boiled wool,
breasts bibbed in heirloom silver
from safeboxes pulled

open Easter week,
sit with their men—small versions
of them squeezed between.

In an aisle seat
that smells of last night's smokes and
hints of aquavit,

I witness the scene:
ghost-gowned for confirmation,
an altar of teens

agree to follow
Luther's creed in a land where
traditions are slow

to become unmoored
from bewitching northern lights,
folktales, and fjords.

## Scenes from Zagreb

Not even a country can rescue Tosca
from the fate of a castle leap that's lethal
here in Croatia's ornate house of opera.

This is a city with a bullet-ridden hospital
and old churches where euro amateurs
are done with death and war's upheaval.

Calvary's purple gentians blister
the hill of bones where widows of war pray
at graves graced with oranges sweet and bitter.

Twig dolls in Jasmine's boutique sway
like sticks of cinnamon in a dance revue,
tiny trinkets for tourists to pack away.

At Petra's Retro Café, hipsters dip into
crackled leather barber chairs and crown
coffee with cream or quaff the local brew.

On a street of cobbles in the capital's old town
is the quirky *Museum of Broken Relationships*—
resting place of come-hither renown

for a spiked heel, strapped and black, slipped
off by an ex-dominatrix from Amsterdam
here for a solo weekend shopping trip.

## Vancouver Hatchery

Slabs of rosy-sided trout billow and bloom in rain-dimpled freshwater pools. Polarized glasses you keep in the Mazda's glove box help us see into the aquatic deep. Close enough to fear, an endless train of container cars races toward Seattle and beyond. What is it that people want? Fertilizer wet or dry, ethanol, appliances, field crops, clothes? The grandchildren want only to scoop a mix of crushed insects and crustaceans from a wooden box, arc it into the sky over the chain-link fence, and watch thick braids of fish go after it.

## Anticipation

My closet's favorite things—their arms raised
    *Please, please, please!*—
are begging for a chance to be rolled,
    to come along in my carry-on.
Beneath my clothes
    are packs of cinnamon Trident,
Red Sox caps, and Pop Rocks candy
    for our French friends.
It's what they've asked for.
    Only mid-March and my head turns French blue.
My mind's a dither.
    I check the flight, and their email begins to pulse.
Our mouths meet at a kitchen table in Nantes.
    The four of us conjure an amazing meal of oysters, octopus,
    mackerel, champagne, and old, hard, salty, orange cheese.
    *Bien sûr!* Another bottle on the table.
Pears. *Merci.* Camembert. *Merci.*
    Sancerre. *Merci. Oui,* the pretty glasses.
The tulips. *Merci.* The petals. *Oui.*
    We shed our scarves because evening is wafting warm.
We will not regret. We are "La Vie en Rose,"
    because this is the way to travel with kiss-kiss friends:
forks in the ragout, the frenzy of tasting,
    the shared joy of discovery.

## Picking Concord Grapes

To disturb a branch with my elbow
was to set off a hail of willing fruit—
a broken strand of royal pearls
lost in the airless mash beneath.

The late August riches surrounded
three sides of a field where boys
hung 'round until enough were ready
for a pickup game with ball and bat.

I was in a frenzy filling plastic pails,
my jeans a purple riot at the knees,
hauling more than my share to put up
jelly the way my great-grandmother did.

You may think me greedy,
but it satisfied a need to work by myself
in the wild bushes, to do a job no one else
in the neighborhood had thought to try.

## Garter Snake

She must have slipped through the open door
       on that cool September morning,
her skin supple, sheeny
       in shades of old-world aubergine.
She was kneeling on a platter of silver sun—
       a supplicant on my dining room rug—
head raised, eyes keen, mouth open
       as if to ask a sensible question.
I was alone, on my own.
Leaning in, I grasped her gently—
a flower singled out for picking.
Her body, all lightness and agility,
wrapped itself around my arm.
With her tail she tested my skin—
like a gardener tamping seeds in a pot of soil.
Outside I released her by the fence,
closed the door and scrubbed my hands.

## My Friend and I

Drive to this garden of wildflowers
set around a glacial pond,
the heavenly opposite of thirst.
Water shinnies down crystal ropes.
We walk on a path of crushed stone.
There are asters and lady slippers.
There is yarrow. So much in bloom.
We pause to hear a herd of sudden rain
stampede across our raised umbrellas.
Ferns lick the wet air,
wanting more of what they already have.
We speak loudly to be heard,
*Look, witch hazel. Look, iris.*
*Look, white violets.*
There are voices beyond.
We are not alone. They are not alone.
We follow them—the spiderwort, I mean,
the moss, the turtles on a log—
until we are where we began,
where we disappear in the parking lot.

## Praise Song

Praise the long way to the beach.
The waves that stand on end
like hair spiked in a barber's chair.
The dinosaur roar of breakers rearing up for shore.

Praise legal fluke. The skilled knife. The copper skillet.
Praise everyone's easy side.
The dog hair everywhere.

The fry of see-through shrimp that skate inside
their box of glass, elbows bent behind their backs.

Praise lemon chickens dreaming on the spit.
The hummingbirds that belly up to the feeder and
lick the sweet stuff from the hourglass.

The dishwasher. Praise him. Praise her.

The color-coded scavenger hunters who end
at the birdbath, splashes of satisfaction in their hands.

Praise the dark that comes when it is called.
Praise grandchildren rapt by fireworks leaping in the yard.

## On the Metro-North from New Haven

Thank God the rain held off. Thank God for May,
　　　　the good coffee, the shuttle that came on time,
a window seat facing southeast with a double wall outlet,
　　　　the way the penciled eyebrows of the woman across from me
rise like index fingers bowing to each other,
　　　　the way the restroom door slides shut without a hand,
the way the man in athletic black bends low over his phone
　　　　as if paying a deep obeisance to an unseen deity—
perhaps the god of thunderbolts and rain,
　　　　or could he be withdrawing money from his 401K
to pay the next installment on his daughter's braces—
　　　　the way the car becomes a quiet keep as it coasts
into Old Greenwich—or is it Riverside, or perhaps Cos Cob,
　　　　Cos Cob, *the town where all good stuff happens.*
At last we unpack at Grand Central Terminal
　　　　like avocados perfectly ripe and ready to eat.
Under a Grecian sky I gaze up at Aquarius of Troy,
　　　　Zeus's anointed water boy tilting a gold cup,
both hands cradling its bowl as he pours stars all over us.

## Imagination

He dips toast into the center of a dropped egg.
She hears the yolk on her plate say, *Don't eat me.*
After breakfast they ferret out a large
cardboard box that becomes a home within a home,
a house without a mortgage or leaky faucets,
a place to move into and out of, like tomorrow.
He uncovers a string of white lights, tapes it to the paper
ceiling. *Where's an outlet, Grammy? Found it!*
He caches books, slithers himself inside.
The only voice is the rain playing hard on the roof.
She clips a reading lamp to the skylight on her end,
thinks to add a flowery scarf. *Presto!* The transformation
from empty to occupied is complete.
The children work in pajamas, unaware of each other or me.
Their dad off to a conference, their mom at work.
I drink tea while they scissor, fold, pencil, paper, paste.
This house with its temporary walls contains everything
real and true—all that glitters and glows in their abode,
everything that matters between breakfast and lunch.

## Root Canal

My car inhales back roads. I want it over with. I want
to be at home having a talk with you about what to do.

How to bear up under the news. Jittery taillights ooze
onto the asphalt ahead, anxious to get a move on.

It's 8 a.m. Snow masks everything except the street.
34 degrees feels like bumping into an old friend.

Rhododendron buds are green as swollen knots.
Sparrows all aflutter are annoyed at running late.

Like dueling instruments in skillful hands, wiper blades
compete by the rules. Fog wraps its soothing arms

around whole trees. I swing into a dry spot, climb salted
concrete stairs. Wet soles stamp the cold tiles in the entryway.

My puffy black coat swallows the metal hook.
Someone calls my name.

## Mohs Surgery, or Gentle on My Mind

I practiced dying laid out on my back,
hands across my chest, heavenly blue cloth

over my eyes, a band in scrubs hovering above.
Tailor-like, the surgeon flapped a piece of skin

across my chin. While country twanged on her
mobile phone, she gave us her best Tammy Wynette.

Stitch by stitch, trying not to flinch, I barely
breathed. One tear slid down my cheek

beyond my reach, good for nothing at all.
I never left that room to soar back to the grass

banking of childhood, where I might have stayed,
playing Giant Steps with my friends until

the streetlights came on, because it was over
just when I was beginning to get the hang of it.

# THREE

## Imagine That

I'm familiar with enough. I own it.
The half-full coffee cup is attractive,
microwaveable, and worth repeating,

like the habendum clause
referring to moveable property:
something to have and to hold.

The breakfast dishes will get done.
There are olives, cheese, and chicken pie
for when I begin to feel that noontime slide.

The plumber fixed the mixing valve
restricting the flow in the bathroom tub.
Now our water is hot again. Imagine that.

If all else fails, I can expect you home after
your appointment with Tina the audiologist,
who will give your aids a high fidelity tune-up.

We'll cut into grilled pork chops together
while I tell you I saw Angie at the library.
You'll ask me how her girls are doing

and, before I can answer, while removing
your plate, you'll remind me that the credit
card payment is due at the end of the month.

## Day before Thanksgiving

Everything annual froze last night.
The cuffs of my sweater
stained with cranberry must,
skins and juice and sticks.
White subway tile measled in red.
Everything raised except the dead.
Where are they when you need them?
If you want it, get it yourself.

## *Therapy*

Tied-up.    Without diamonds.    A cappella.
With fish in mind.    With fingers for forks.
With edible violets.    With long-wooden-spooning.
With hand-pecked instructions.    Elbows rolling.
Palms pushing back in a wake of white dust.
Riding the waves.    Yesterday's loaves.    To beat the band.
Mistakes boiled down in aluminum clad.    Against the grain.
Guided by uncorseted crones in housedresses and hairnets.
With a dash of authenticity.    Emptying bottles.
Squeezing cheesecloth.    By the seat of my pants.
Bowled over by red-hot induction.    The daily edition.
Nothing parsley can't fix.    No one's the wiser.

## Spring Chaos

The Weber is grill-still, front teeth cracked,
upturned legs airing indecently on the flagstone,
a mark of last week's violent spent wind.
Our neighbor says his dock got knocked off, lost,
bonded with the bottom of the pond.

Some things lie suffering until they're spied,
like the skylight frame that's fraying paint,
the water damage seen when spring sun seeps in.
Like your stomach spotted behind your heart—
canned goods boxing pasta for cabinet space.

Your doctors say some things will have to change.
Organs need pulling down, stitched and rearranged.
I gulp a green iron pill, breathe black tea
and sentence penciled worries to wither
inside a Chinese vase, jay blue and miniscule.

## Talking to Nature

From my kitchen's barricade, its stock-in-trade,
I run, hide outside in the wood's deep cool
with moss that cloaks like velvet cloth,
with a jay who taunts from out of sight—
*You're it, you're it*—with walls of stone
still bickering about whose side they own,
with a bumblebee in his azalea dream,
a caterpillar in my hair, rain, all green,
fairy-tale dark at 4 o'clock and with you,
good mud, your pants all covered with mirth.
I hear that it will be over soon;
I hear that it won't be over soon.
But that's not your concern.

## The NewsHour

August and more prevention to swallow,
like July, June, May, April and March before that.
We worked hard today cleaning the garage—keeps us on our feet.
Maybe it will earn us some travel rewards.
How I miss those penciled plans, the rush of strange and far away.
Oh, just get me a glass of Hendrick's on ice;
I'll drag a lawn chair out and down it in the driveway.
The hose is bleeding onto the street.
How bedraggled spring was this year.
All that rain. All those broadleaf intruders.
No more kids ringing the doorbell with
bags of oranges and grapefruit to hawk.
Look! There's a groundhog on his toes
like a bear in the green grass of home.
It's time for *The NewsHour*.
Come, let's watch. It won't be nutritious,
but dinner will be right out of the oven and
might end with something brief and spectacular,
something sweet that goes down easy.

## Aubade

—after Marianne Moore

Eggs boiling in a pot,
      tapping their toes and heels
      to a breakfast reel.

Feeding on chilly air,
      orchids like moon-white moths
      take in their daily broth.

I convince myself to
      head out there on my own,
      beyond a couple grown

old like me. I stroll way
      beyond the fence painter,
      beyond the surveyor,

taking in the happenings:
      a house with a new peak,
      low tide's seaweed reek,

solitude found in the
      splendor of busyness,
      the comfort of sameness.

An hour disappears
      like that quiet reynard
      I blinked in someone's yard.

What propels me home is
      a day that's still wound up,
      a glimmer that won't corrupt.

Tomato plant blossoms,
      mint crawling here and there,
      the shed in disrepair.

## Finding Love in the Laundry Room

When I was old enough, I walked to North Park's
fishpond full of hungry carp and swings to dream on.

I walked to the bookmobile across from the fire barn
and lugged home hardcover fiction I never finished.

I moved to the city and walked along Bay State Road
to night classes in education that gave me migraines.

Then I found you in the basement laundry room
of our apartment building in Waltham, your sleeves

rolled back two cuff lengths. You were folding undershirts
with those hands I longed to know the backs and palms of.

I was jealous of those V-necks that you pulled over
your head, that touched your high cheek bones

and the divot in your chin—cloth that obeyed, lay soft
against your chest, your flat belly, your straight back.

Somewhere in my brain I could hear the hot rivets
on your jeans clicking their tongues in the dryer

as we stood close, alone no more, the top-loader
shuddering as its insides spun out of control.

That was fifty years ago. Today I walk along
the ocean road and come home to find you

in your favorite bleach-stained jeans, their placket
splattered white where I spilled drops of Clorox.

You sit over a spill of chrome-plated sockets,
fondling each hefty jewel in your left hand,

as your eyes scan the custom-molded storage box
for the designated slot you will slip it into.

## End of Wandering

Cutlery's music has ceased, spirits locked away,
no brogue-word overheard in that grand Killarney dining room

where we devoured salmon every possible way for a week.
In Rhode Island, May is rain-soft, the ocean agreeable—

gulls line up on the sand like white bowling pins,
two women arm-in-arm giggle like nuns on an outing,

a cardinal takes off like a burning shuttlecock
thwacked on the sweet spot of a badminton racket.

Without warning, I recall *Still Life with Wine Goblet and Oysters*
waiting for me on the wall at Boston's MFA,

a goblet transparent with dusk, a knife askew,
its pewter handle a cold grip and oysters shivering on ice,

ready for the slurp. Beyond the gold frame,
a chair is overturned and a merchant is missing.

Then everything shut down. It was the last time
I went anyplace, traveled anywhere.

## Who I Am

I want to remember my imaginary friend Mary,
then call her in from where I left her in the street
when I was five, before she gets run over again.

I want to remember my grandmother calling me
*a brazen hussy, a proud haughty* when she caught me
preening in her bedroom mirror.

I want to remember when I wished my name was Deirdre,
wished for a night at Billy Bob's Fort Worth honky tonk
stomping in my straight-legged jeans and killer cowgirl boots.

I want to remember to shinny into my aqua St. John knit
when I'm 80, the one with the gold belt buckle that clicks shut,
the one I bought for my 40th.

I want to remember the fine powder of anticipation, how it clings
to everything that's vital and worth being bad for.

I want to remember that you are the only one, you with your
left handedness and shirts with a pocket over your heart.

I want to remember being out there with Mary, feet bare,
lifting the hems of our sundresses to catch a summer shower
as it dashes down, noisy and necessary.

## Sitting at the Beach

as an egg splits open the morning orange
and drizzles across the bay.

The waves' teeth grind
the carcasses of once-living things.

My ears fill with sea static—a radio dialing
for news of the world. Is anyone there?

The hiss inhabits my mind,
a sound more soothing than sense,

each finishing fetch a mesmerizing murmur,
a sonic blue pulse that belongs here.

Hazy and haughty. I'll take the memory
to the grave on my back.

The art of silent sitting is a rock at low tide
strung with purple-backed mussels.

There's enough ocean for everyone,
like getting an invitation to a beach party

we can all walk to. Where we tote our own
IPA and carry in small bags of Cheetos.

Nothing to share but ourselves.
It counts for something.

I devour every salty bite,
lick the dust from my fingers.

*This Present Life*

hangs
off-kilter.
      Good God, our parks have ceased to be parks.
      Sawhorses with orange
            and white striped signs warn us away.
So
it goes as
      trains disappear from appointed stops.
      Commuters button up
            as the weather turns nasty and
rain
falls on lots
      cars used to circle for open spots.
      No copters reporting
            *stop and go* on the radio.
Ech-
os invade
      where kids once rushed hell-bent to lunchrooms,
      flush with commotion and
            cliques bunched up elbow to elbow.
I
count fewer
      reasons to look up into the sky,
      to wish on a jet's wing
            for a sprayed-clean seat heading east.

Good
times have been
      X'd out. Summer is a washout too.
      Bespattered Newport jazz.
            Ferries stock-still against the dock.
I'm
primed for some
      hot-damn sun-drenched days shot with sequins
      and beaded pearls, oyster
            bars, chlorine pools—the things I miss.

My
friend tells me
     Lebanese women love their bangles.
     I need reasons to dance,
          to jangle gold on both wrists.


                   —after Marianne Moore

## Looking Back

The policeman is here. I'm five in braids.
The officer doesn't see me. The landlady shook,
shook, shook her dust mop over laundry my mother hung
from our first-floor porch. I'm invisible. Hiding in place.

Seventy years on, the sheets are still wet on the line.
The calm man in blue hasn't left.
Potatoes boil on the stove. Her sobs are audible.

Now in this spring of disguise and wait, I think
if life ends in a cough and a sweat, there is so much to lose.
No need to walk back into that kitchen.

The chances of loss accumulate: the sadness of rust,
the futility of longing, the stupidity of chewing gum,
the freedom of seeds, fingers that don't add up.

I'm masked. Alert for headache, shortness of breath,
lungs filling up. The kettle is calling. The sausage is thawing.

## Women Friends

There you are, scooping out summer from
a tin can campground in the dunes of Provincetown.
        Spreading a slather of cottage cheese
to the far edges of buttered toast.
        Pawing through the trash for a lost gold bracelet—
or was it two silver spoons?
        With a straight face, you claimed that dust
was mahogany's protective crust.
        You hurled teacups at the wall when the old Singer
went zigzag instead of straight.
        Your collection of huddled perfume bottles was
like a convention of flamingos gabbling at the shore.
        I reach back for all of you: those who bird,
those who can't fold a map, those who never
        breathe a word, the mistress of grammar,
the ones who stopped going to church, and those
        who believe in Herbes de Provence.
Without you, there would be no pazazz,
        no dazzling glass rings, no speeding tickets,
no weddings with lopsided cakes,
        no kick of nasturtium along with the gin.

## Acknowledgments

Many thanks to the editors of the following publications where these poems first appeared, some with different titles and slight changes to the original versions.

*Amethyst Review:* "Grace"
*Ars Medica:* "Inheritance"
*Atlanta Review:* "Garter Snake"
*CALYX Magazine:* "Scenes from Zagreb"
*Cider Press Review:* "The Chaos of Spring," "I'm Talking to You," "Possibility"
*The Examined Life Journal:* "Room 431"
*The Healing Muse:* "Mohs Surgery, or Gentle on My Mind"
*Indolent Press:* "What Keeps Me Going"
*The Lake:* "A Natural," "Easter Morning," "Heirloom"
*The Lyric Magazine:* "Pentecost Sunday in Norway"
*The Galway Review:* "Great-Aunts," "Sitting on the Beach"
*The Moth Magazine:* "April Escape," "Praise Song"
*The New York Times Metropolitan Diary:* "In a Downpour"
*One Art:* "Imagine That"
*Persimmon Tree:* "Picking Concord Grapes," "Paris"
*Poetry Quarterly:* "Wonder"
*Rat's Ass Review:* "Wedding Day Photo," "Allied Bombs Hit Foe in France Hard," "Evening Bag," "Leave-Taking"
*Rockvale Review:* "Imagination"
*Southwest Review:* "Lost Landscapes"
*Sparks of Calliope:* "My Friend and I," "Who I Am"
*Tar River Review:* "Root Canal"
*Thimble Literary Review:* "Women Friends"
*The Worcester Review:* "The Long Ride," "End of Childhood," "Scent of Lilacs"

I want to acknowledge my gratitude to the Fine Arts Work Center for classes taught by Rowan Richardo Phillips, Kristina Marie Darling, Tyler Mills, and Erin Belieu, and to the Lexington Community Education Program. All these poetry encounters have helped me grow as a poet.

Most of all I owe deep gratitude to Tom Daley, outstanding poet and teacher exemplar, without whose support and guidance this book would not have been possible.

I am indebted to my fellow workshop poets, both past and present, for their perceptive insights, encouragement, and friendship. Thanks also to Ann Taylor for her careful proofreading of the manuscript.

I am also grateful to Heather Treseler for her support and for sharing her knowledge of all things poetry; to Virginia Konchan for her amazing manuscript review; to Sandy Raymond, Director of the Wayland Public Library, for her enthusiastic endorsement of my book; and to family members who have been first readers and helpful critics. Thank you all.

In the end, this book would not have become a reality without the remarkable talent, dedication, and care of Diane Kistner, Director and Editor/Publisher of FutureCycle Press.

## About FutureCycle Press

FutureCycle Press is dedicated to publishing lasting English-language poetry in both print-on-demand and Kindle formats. Founded in 2007 by long-time independent editor/publishers and partners Diane Kistner and Robert S. King, the press was incorporated as a nonprofit in 2012. A number of our editors are distinguished poets and writers in their own right, and we have been actively involved in the small press movement going back to the early seventies.

Each year, we award the FutureCycle Poetry Book Prize and honorarium for the best original full-length volume of poetry we published that year. Introduced in 2013, proceeds from our Good Works projects are donated to charity. Our Selected Poems series highlights contemporary poets with a substantial body of work to their credit; with this series we strive to resurrect work that has had limited distribution and is now out of print.

We are dedicated to giving all of the authors we publish the care their work deserves, offering a catalog of the most diverse and distinguished work possible, and paying forward any earnings to fund more great books. All of our books are kept "alive" and available unless and until an author requests a title be taken out of print.

We've learned a few things about independent publishing over the years. We've also evolved a unique and resilient publishing model that allows us to focus mainly on vetting and preserving for posterity poetry collections of exceptional quality without becoming overwhelmed with bookkeeping and mailing, fundraising activities, or taxing editorial and production "bubbles." To find out more about what we are doing, come see us at futurecycle.org.

## *The FutureCycle Poetry Book Prize*

All original, full-length poetry books published by FutureCycle Press in a given calendar year are considered for the annual FutureCycle Poetry Book Prize. This allows us to consider each submission on its own merits, outside of the context of a traditional contest. Too, the judges see the finished book, which will have benefitted from the beautiful book design and strong editorial gloss we are famous for.

The book ranked the best in judging is announced as the prize-winner in January of the subsequent year. There is no fixed monetary award; instead, the winning poet receives an honorarium of 20% of the total net royalties from all poetry books and chapbooks the press sold online in the year the winning book was published. The winner is also accorded the honor of being on the panel of judges for the next year's competition; all judges receive copies of the contending books to keep for their personal library.

Made in United States
Orlando, FL
05 March 2023